THE LIBRARY OF CONGRESS

THE LOUIS CHARLES ELSON MEMORIAL FUND

DISCREPANCIES IN HAYDN BIOGRAPHIES

A LECTURE DELIVERED BY

ANTHONY van HOBOKEN

THE LIBRARY OF CONGRESS

THE LOUIS CHARLES ELSON MEMORIAL FUND

DISCREPANCIES IN HAYDN BIOGRAPHIES

A LECTURE DELIVERED BY

ANTHONY van HOBOKEN

Dr. Phil. honoris causa, Christian-Albrechts-Universität, Kiel
Dr. honoris causa, Rijksuniversiteit, Utrecht

IN

THE WHITTALL PAVILION

OF THE LIBRARY OF CONGRESS

MAY 18, 1962

Translated by Donald Mintz

Washington : 1962

L.C. Card 62–64846

LOUIS CHARLES ELSON was born on April 17, 1848, and died on February 14, 1920. He was educated in Boston, his native city, and in Germany. As a teacher at the New England Conservatory of Music and as music editor for Boston newspapers, he exerted a great influence for music in this country over a period of many years. He also served as musical correspondent for several European and South American papers, and he enjoyed distinction as a lecturer to the public as well as in the classroom. As author, composer, and editor, he had a career of great significance in America's musical development.

In 1945 the Library of Congress received a bequest from the late Mrs. Bertha L. Elson, widow of Louis Charles Elson, to provide lectures on music and musical literature in memory of her husband. Dr. van Hoboken's lecture was one of the series made possible by Mrs. Elson's generous bequest, which also supplied funds for this publication.

DISCREPANCIES
IN
HAYDN BIOGRAPHIES

A NYONE WHO READS a Haydn biography of some scope will soon notice that the greater part of the book is not about Haydn himself. The reader will find detailed descriptions of persons and circumstances that have only a loose connection with Haydn—if indeed they have any at all! The recounting of Haydn's life is the smallest portion of these biographies—and this portion, in turn, is 75 percent anecdotal.

As a matter of fact, we do not really know very much about Haydn's life. And it is remarkable how many of the sources concerned with it—sources parts of which older biographers were able to employ—have been lost. A few examples will suffice. The Weimar collection used by Gerber at the beginning of the nineteenth century was burned in 1825. A collection belonging to the Bishops of Passau was similarly destroyed by fire some years earlier. "A Traveler" writing in the *Allgemeine musikalische Zeitung* in 1827 claimed to have seen a large number of opera scores in Eisenstadt, but today only a small quantity of such scores can still be found in the Esterházy Archives, which have since been moved to Budapest. The holdings of Lippe-Detmold, which Brahms diligently studied, have subsequently vanished from the face of the earth, and the Breitkopf Collection, of which Pohl made exhaustive use for his biography of Haydn, likewise no longer exists.

Fortunately, there has survived an autobiographical sketch, written by Haydn at Esterháza Castle on July 6, 1776. There are two extant autographs of this document. One is located in the Szechényi Library in Budapest; the other, a fair copy of the first, is in my library. There is a third copy in Budapest, but it is not in Haydn's hand. Excerpts from this sketch were inaccurately published in 1778 in the periodical *Das gelehrte Österreich*. It was not until 1836 that the *Wiener Zeitschrift für Literatur und Mode* published it in its entirety, but this publication was based on a vanished copy which did not correspond exactly with the original. In this form the sketch was taken over by Pohl and printed (1878) in the appendix to the first volume of his biography of Haydn.

The autobiographical sketch at least gives us some information about Haydn's youth, but this early document obviously can tell us nothing about the crucial later period of the composer's life. Haydn's letters, insofar as they have survived, are as silent about this period as are the London notebooks, which are restricted to events of the years directly in question.

Through more recent research in the Esterházy Archives in Budapest, letters from the 1760's and 70's have been found and published. These give us an idea of the obligations placed on Haydn in connection with his position as *Kapellmeister*, but for more biographical details we depend primarily on reminiscences which Haydn, as an old man, considered sufficiently noteworthy to be transmitted.

These reminiscences were first told to Georg August Griesinger, secretary of the embassy of the Electorate of Saxony in Vienna. As Griesinger himself writes, he had the good fortune to have maintained an unbroken relationship with and to have been honored with the confidence of Joseph Haydn in the last years of the master's life. This was possible because, from 1799 on, Griesinger acted as business agent for the Leipzig music publishers, Breitkopf and Härtel, in their dealings with Haydn. Griesinger's recollections of what Haydn told him first appeared in 1809 in the *Allgemeine musikalische Zeitung* and then, a year later, in book form as *Biographische Notizen über Joseph Haydn*. His description became a foundation of Haydn research and was newly reprinted a few years ago.

The biographical notes of Albert Christian Dies follow directly those of Griesinger. According to his own testimony Dies, a landscape artist, poet, and musician, paid homage as a dilettante to more than one muse. He visited Haydn between 1805 and 1808. At first Haydn parried with the comment that "his life story could not be of interest to anyone." This remark, perhaps, attacks by innuendo the writing of high-toned autobiographies, a product which was then becoming fashionable. But Haydn nevertheless admitted his admirer, and the *Biographische Nachrichten von Joseph Haydn*,

2

nach muendlichen Erzaehlungen desselben entworfen und herausgegeben von Albert Christoph Dies resulted from these visits. Dies' delineation is far more artful and sensitive than Griesinger's, and it is unjust that less attention is paid to it. It, too, has recently been reissued.

It is not uninteresting to consider the reciprocal effect of these two biographies. In 1806, when Dies asked Haydn to whom he should submit his work, Haydn referred him to Griesinger. After he had made the latter's acquaintance, Dies wrote that for several years Griesinger, without Haydn's knowledge, had been quietly assembling material for a biography of the master, which means that Griesinger did not question Haydn as Dies had done. At whatever time Griesinger may have seen Dies' manuscript describing his first visit with Haydn, it is entirely plausible that he used it for his final biography. As I shall show later, by 1806 he had hardly gotten past the very beginnings. Dies, on the other hand, mentions Griesinger's series of articles in the *Allgemeine musikalische Zeitung,* which he found especially useful for the description of Haydn's earlier development.

Comparison of these two biographies shows that, in general, what they have to tell us about Haydn's youth coincides fairly well with Haydn's own report. When they are not always consonant with one another regarding the later periods, I am convinced this is due, to a considerable extent, to the different temperaments of the two biographers, which, in turn, may have caused Haydn to become freer and more communicative with one than the other.

I should now like to adduce several examples to show the extent to which these two biographies agree, disagree, and supplement one another in reporting a number of individual events. Many episodes that one reads about in these two books were not only taken over but were even extended by later biographers.

Discrepancies begin directly with Haydn's childhood. Griesinger tells us how the young Haydn accompanied the singing of his parents on an imaginary violin with such rhythmic accuracy that they decided he had musical talent and sent him to a cousin in Hainburg for further training. Haydn himself reports in his autobiographical

3

sketch that as a boy of five he could correctly repeat all his father's simple songs. This was surely the better proof of his musical talent and certainly the source of the quotations of the folksongs in the works he wrote in London so far from his home. Griesinger confirms this when he writes that the melodies of these songs had engraved themselves so deeply in Haydn's memory that he still remembered them in his latest years. This must have been the talent that caused his father to send the boy to his relative, the headmaster Frank in Hainburg. Three years later, continues Griesinger, the choirmaster of St. Stephen's in Vienna, Georg Reutter the younger, on a tour looking for new choir boys, visited Hainburg, examined young Haydn in sight-singing, and offered him a handful of cherries. Dies' report is similar, but he gives no date and has Reutter presenting the boy a coin.

In the first volume of his Haydn biography, Carl Ferdinand Pohl describes a touching farewell scene in which Haydn's seven-year-old sister beholds her five-year-old brother in an almost ceremonious fashion, while the father, turned towards the worried mother, gestures in the direction of a cradle prepared for the reception of a new offspring. Since Joseph had become five on March 31, 1737, and his brother Michael was born on September 13 of that year, this farewell must have taken place toward the end of August 1737. In his book about Haydn's ancestors, Ernst Fritz Schmid corrects this by pointing out that Joseph was present at the baptism of his brother on September 14.

Accordingly, Haydn's father would have gone with him to Hainburg at about the time when, even today, children in rural areas first go to school, namely, after the end of the summer's work in the fields. And so those fantasies collapse, fantasies according to which Haydn went through the fields of ripe grain, through the *Heidentor* near Petronell, and on to Hainburg while the happy lark chirped above him. The more sober version, however, agrees with the autobiographical sketch, in which Haydn reports how, in his seventh year, he boldly sang several masses from the choirloft in Hainburg. Both biographers leave Haydn in Hainburg until the end of his

4

eighth year, that is, April 1740, when he went to the choir school of St. Stephen's in Vienna. But while, in Griesinger's view, Haydn received his discharge at the age of 17 because his voice broke, Dies has him remain at the choir school until the age of 18.

Haydn himself says of his time at the choir school that he learned a good deal and that he sang soprano until his eighteenth year when he finally lost his voice. Correspondingly, Dies writes that when the Empress Maria Theresa heard the boys in Klosterneuberg on the Feast of St. Leopold she said that Haydn no longer sang, but cawed! As Haydn became 18 in March 1750, this event must have occurred on November 15, 1749, and he must have been discharged shortly thereafter.

The anecdote of the ominous castration that Reutter is supposed to have urged on Haydn in order to preserve his voice is reported only by Griesinger. According to the story, Haydn received the suggestion with unmitigated joy until, by chance, his father intervened. Griesinger specifically notes that he did not hear the story from Haydn himself but learned it from a third person. This third person was presumably Pleyel, who spread abroad a good deal of incorrect information about Haydn but left no writings concerning him.

The two biographers come together again in the depiction of a pilgrimage which Haydn is said to have made to Mariazell. When, on applying to the choirmaster of the church, he was denied permission to sing in the choir there, he is supposed unhesitatingly to have bribed the soloist, torn the music from his hand, and sung so beautifully that the attention of everyone was drawn to him. The chapter is supposed to have boarded him for a week and even to have given him money for his return to Vienna.

How that episode can be brought into agreement with the breaking of his voice, which was the cause of his discharge from St. Stephen's, is not explained, and it is still arousing confusion in the mind of the modern biographer. There is another discrepancy regarding the time of this pilgrimage. Griesinger has Haydn undertake it shortly after his departure from the choir school; Dies, however, places it in the following spring. In his book on Haydn's

5

Masses, Carl Maria Brand tells us that, in general, pilgrims first came to Mariazell in July, and that it was by no means unusual for the needy among them to be boarded gratis.

Haydn himself writes little about the years after his departure from St. Stephen's. In his autobiographical sketch we are merely told that he composed diligently but without a secure foundation, until he finally had the good fortune to learn the true basis of composition from the famous maestro Porpora, that he later obtained a position as music director to Count Morzin on the recommendation of Baron von Fürnberg, and that from there he went to the position of *Kapellmeister* in the service of Prince Esterházy.

Apparently it was with the greatest pleasure that Haydn told his visitors about the composition of his first opera, *Der krumme Teufel,* which he wrote for the comedian Kurz-Bernardon. Here again we encounter a discrepancy. Griesinger writes that Haydn was 19 years old when he composed the opera; Dies places the work in Haydn's twenty-first year. The opera, unfortunately, has disappeared. And though Griesinger writes further of the pleasure with which Haydn loitered before the shops of the music dealers where one or another of his works was displayed in print, these prints, too, have not yet been rediscovered. To be sure, Haydn, as he later confesses, had given away many autographs which could then have been copied and sold; yet such early copies are also unknown to Haydn researchers.

We read in Dies how Haydn acquired Carl Philipp Emanuel Bach's *Versuch ueber die wahre Art das Clavier zu spielen.* This could have been as early as 1753, since the first part of the book appeared in that year. Dies is the only one who mentions Haydn's opinions about Mattheson's *Der vollkommene Capellmeister* and Fux' *Gradus ad Parnassum.* The German translation of the latter had been available since 1742. But Dies also offers Haydn's views on Kirnberger's writings, which did not appear until much later and which Haydn could not have studied at that time. The judgment falls without reservation in favor of C. P. E. Bach.

A little-known event was reported in the *Neue Berliner Musikzeitung* under the title "Blosse Füsse und seidene Strümpfe." According to the story, Haydn was polishing Porpora's boots when, through the open window, he heard Regina Mingotti sing one of his arias. Now, Mingotti could very well have been in Vienna, traveling from an engagement in Dresden to another in Madrid. She could surely have visited her old teacher and director, Nicolo Porpora, who at the age of 65 had been pensioned on January 1, 1752, and had moved to Vienna. An aria by Haydn is certainly conceivable at that time and indeed is mentioned by Wendschuh in his dissertation on Haydn's operas. But the question is whether Haydn would have found it necessary to polish Porpora's boots—which Dies also refers to—or otherwise to be Porpora's servant, as, for example, during the excursion to Mannersdorf. We know from Ernst Fritz Schmid's book about the master's ancestors that Haydn's father was by no means to be counted among the poorest inhabitants of the village of Rohrau. He had been a market judge since 1741, and by 1749 he was a farmer who had considerable land holdings. From Jančik's biography of Michael Haydn, we know of a letter from the father in which he announces that he will send a carriage to Vienna so that Michael, Joseph, and a friend can come to Rohrau. One might well think that he was also in a position to protect his son in Vienna from the direst poverty.

But aside from this, we read again and again of other sources of income that Joseph possessed. A businessman named Buchholz lent him 150 Gulden, and by 1751 Haydn was in a position to repay him. He gave music lessons for which he received first two and later five Gulden. This and the admittedly small sums he received as an organist in various chapels could have brought him perhaps the same annual sum that Reutter received for each choirboy, a sum on which he could have been able to live. In any case, he brought savings of 1,000 Gulden to his marriage in 1760. Yet in the last year of his life Haydn emphasized over and over to visitors that he had had a very difficult youth.

In this period there is also mention of a Countess Thun who saw Haydn's early sonatas and thereupon sent for him and gave him 25 ducats. The person in question here is probably Philippine Aloisia von Thun, the widow of Count Johann Franz Joseph von Thun-

7

Hohenstein, *née* von Harrach. As a fourth-degree cousin of Count Karl Anton von Harrach, she had good reason for concerning herself about the young man who was born on her cousin's estate. She is not, however, the Countess Thun referred to by Pohl and who, according to Count Zinsendorf's diary, played a Haydn Sonata in 1775.

With regard to the rest of the time in Vienna, Dies mentions the friendship of Haydn and Dittersdorf, who together played many a merry prank. It is striking that on one occasion Dies describes an incident in which Dittersdorf, who was seven and a half years younger, physically protected the older Haydn. Dittersdorf says nothing about this in his autobiography, where he mentions his connection with Haydn as having first occurred in 1763.

Griesinger, for his part, tells of Baron von Fürnberg at whose house Haydn played quartets and also composed his own first string quartet. Griesinger gives the date 1750 for the latter event. This is definitely too early. Then an admittedly quasi-legendary figure, Major Weirach, who fell into Austrian captivity during the Seven Years' War, offered a judgment on the first quartets. According to the original document, the Major heard them at the home of the nobleman on whose estates Haydn was born or lived at the time. As a consequence this discrepancy shows that one modern Haydn biographer has the quartets played in Rohrau where Haydn was indeed born in 1732, while another places the event in von Fürnberg's Schloss Weinzierl. Haydn was actually the guest of von Fürnberg in whose residence he composed and played his first quartets.

The two biographers differ also in locating Haydn's quarters. Both agree in mentioning the garret room in the Michaelerhaus, but Griesinger has him move from there to the Seilerstätte where all his worldly possessions were stolen. Dies, on the other hand, takes him to a miserable room in the home of a stocking worker's family, where he met his future father-in-law, the wigmaker Keller.

Haydn's entry upon his duties as *Kapellmeister* to Count Morzin is generally placed in the year 1759. Pohl, however, feels that this date, too, must be considered an assumption. At least the composition of Haydn's first symphony, written while he was in Morzin's service, is placed in this year. The Quartet No. 5 which, supplied with oboes and horns, was originally also a symphony, is evidently not included in this calculation.

We do not regain firm ground until Haydn's marriage to Anna Aloysia Appollonia Keller. This took place at a public ceremony in the presence of witnesses at St. Stephen's Cathedral in November 1760. Accordingly there can be no question of the possibility that the marriage was kept secret from Count Morzin, who wanted only unmarried musicians in his service. Yet this "secret marriage" is common in the biographies. Rather, it should be assumed that, at this time, Morzin had already dissolved or considerably reduced his musical establishment, and that Haydn was no longer in his service. He had not yet taken up his position with Prince Esterházy, for the decree appointing him was signed in Vienna on May 1, 1761. It seems reasonable to assume that this was the period during which Haydn moved to the Kellers. In any case, he did not do so immediately after his discharge from the choir school, as Carpani maintains.

Haydn's rise to fame began in Eisenstadt where the Princes Esterházy resided. In 1766, the same year that Prince Nicolaus inaugurated his new castle, Esterháza, the newspaper *Wiener Diarium* referred to Haydn as "the nation's favorite" and said that he was to music what Gellert was to poetry. Despite this public recognition, little is known about Haydn's daily life during the 30 years he spent at the Esterházy court. Visitors, who were drawn in ever-increasing numbers as Haydn's fame grew, have reported almost nothing about it. Johann Abraham Peter Schulz, who visited Haydn in 1770, makes a touching remark about his piety while at work. Burney, who was in Vienna briefly during his musical journey in the fall of 1772, did not meet Haydn there, nor did he travel to Hungary in order to visit him, although the court of Nicolaus the Magnificent, as well as Haydn himself, already enjoyed international renown. Burney came to know Haydn for the first time years later in London.

Bernhard Schott, a music publisher from Mainz, was among the visitors of the 1770's, but business connections probably did not arise from that meeting, for the first Haydn works published by Schott appeared in the second half of the 1780's, and these are not first editions. Maximilian Stadler—not yet an abbot—visited Haydn in 1781, and remained his friend for life, but he left no memoirs. We learn the most from Michael Kelly, who was a tenor at the Royal Opera in Vienna from 1783 to 1787, and who apparently met Haydn frequently. Kelly met him again in London and once had dinner with him. Since descriptions of Castle Esterháza also contain little about Haydn's daily life, it is not surprising that Haydn biographers so often stray into peripheral areas.

So for the first 60 years of Haydn's life we find ourselves back with the first two biographies, and it is precisely for this period that they are not very productive. Both agree in mentioning the anecdote of the *Farewell Symphony*, as well as the story of the sly poodle. Accordingly, these are to be traced back to Haydn himself. On the other hand, Griesinger tells us of only one fire that occurred in Haydn's house in Eisenstadt, and that manuscripts of operas were lost in it. Here Dies is better informed. Haydn's house burned down twice, first in 1768 and then in July 1776. Prince Nicolaus had it rebuilt both times. Pleyel later said that the autograph of the opera *Armida* was lost in the fire of 1776, and that the work itself survived only because he had previously copied the score in secret. The discrepancy of this story is immediately apparent from the fact that *Armida* was not composed until seven years later. Moreover, Pleyel never copied it, and the original holograph is still extant; a part of it is even in this country.

Haydn sold the house two years later. The biographers do not tell us where he lived after that. If one reads Pohl's description of Haydn's rural life at Castle Esterháza, one assumes that Haydn lived there all year round. The extant letters of the period convey the same impression, for all of them, written in the depth of winter, are dated from Esterháza. Haydn once complained that a letter failed to reach him because it was addressed to Eisenstadt. His continuous residence at Esterháza was possible only so long as the princely household was also in continuous residence and the opera steadily at work. In a recently published book, *Haydn als Opernkapell-meister,* Dr. Dénes Bartha and László Somfai report in detail on Haydn's activities in the opera house. They show how he made arbi-

10

trary cuts in the works to be performed, transposed and altered arias, and from time to time composed his own. This last action was undertaken largely to favor the soprano, Luigia Polzelli, with whom he was very intimate at the time. The book does not contain much about Haydn's working conditions outside of the princely establishment and his occasional appearances as conductor in other cities— Graz and Vienna, for example. In January 1790 a letter is suddenly dated "Vienna, at home." We do not know how long Haydn owned this dwelling or whether his wife, of whom one finds no mention, lived there. She was not likely to have been with him at Esterháza.

The period of Haydn's life following Prince Nicolaus' death is far easier to survey than that during which he was bound exclusively to Eisenstadt and Esterháza. In London he kept the notebooks mentioned earlier, documents of which his first two biographers made advantageous use. The greatest discrepancy between the two lies in the varying transcriptions of an index to the works that Haydn composed in England, which was added to a notebook for the second English journey. This index, which also includes works composed in Vienna between the two trips to England, is given in different versions by the two biographers. While Dies prints the index in English, the language in which one supposes Haydn wrote it, Griesinger translates it into German. His version contains one entry less than that of Dies, but in compensation he adds to each entry the number of pages in the autograph. It can easily be shown, however, from the autographs that are still extant that these page-counts are not correct. In spite of this, later biographers generally take over Griesinger's information. They appear to consider that Griesinger, as the confidant of a large publishing house, was a better hand at figures than the artist Dies. Which version is correct can no longer be shown, for the notebook that allegedly contains the index has been lost.

The third biographer, who published reminiscences of Haydn as if he had heard them from the subject himself, was surely less successful in this respect. Giuseppe Carpani was an active man of letters in Milan, but he was obliged to leave the city when it was

11

entered by the French Revolutionary armies under General Bonaparte. He went to Vienna with Archduke Ferdinand, the Austrian governor of Lombardy. There Emperor Franz entrusted him with the censorship of the theater and paid him an honorarium. At the desire of the Empress, Carpani translated *The Creation* into Italian, and this task no doubt brought him into contact with Haydn. But Haydn did not have sufficient confidence in Carpani to turn to him for the Italian translation of *The Seven Last Words*. While Pohl says that Carpani came and went at Haydn's house, proof is lacking, but we do have such proof for the visits of the Swedish diplomat Silverstolpe, for example. We know from Bertuch, however, who visited Haydn in 1806, that, aside from Griesinger, Dies was among the very few persons the venerable old man saw from time to time.

Carpani's biography, *Le Haydine,* appeared for the first time in 1812. A single fact suffices to show that the letters are supplied with fictitious dates—on September 25, 1811, he complains that he has not heard from Haydn for a long time. Haydn had been dead for more than two years! At the beginning of the biography Carpani drops every name imaginable. This would not have been necessary had he been able to draw on information obtained from Haydn himself. Furthermore, he never even mentions a single Haydn letter. He would certainly have made such reference had it been in his power to do so. Despite Carpani's long residence in Vienna, he could not be said to have mastered the German language, as can be seen in his erroneous transcription of the text of a canon. This is further confirmed by Zelter, who met him in Vienna in 1819. So Haydn would have had to tell his reminiscences to Carpani in Italian!

Carpani seldom calls on Haydn's authority when he is retailing his improbable anecdotes and incidents. And the nicknames he attaches to Haydn's symphonies—names like "Bella Circassa," "Elena Grece," "Solitario," "Persiana," and "Poltrone"—cannot possibly have come from Haydn. Today we do not even know the symphonies to which they refer. Surely Carpani cannot have used any words of Haydn for his literary outpourings about the symphonies.

12

As compensation for all this, he is the first to mention Haydn's friend, the singer Luigia Polzelli, about whom the other early biographers tell us nothing. Yet Carpani cannot have gotten his information about the lady from Haydn himself, for he calls her "Boselli" and maintains that her death was the cause of Haydn's first journey to England in 1790. In reality, Polzelli was still alive as Carpani was writing, and she had nothing whatever to do with Haydn's trip. Towards the end of his biography, when he wishes to coin a special distinction for his hero, Carpani compares him with Field Marshal Loudon and calls them "two illustrious idiots."

Marie Henri Beyle, later known as Stendhal, was the next of Haydn's biographers. His *Lettres écrites de Vienne en Autriche, sur le célèbre compositeur J.ᵉ Haydn,* published under the pseudonym of Louis-Alexandre-César Bombet, is based primarily on Carpani's *Haydine.* Large sections of Carpani's book are translated verbatim into French. Sometimes he shoots past the mark, as for example when he copies from Carpani the supposed fact that he (Beyle) paid Haydn several visits in 1808, whereas Beyle first arrived in Vienna on May 10, 1809, as an officer in Napoleon's army. In this capacity he may have attended Haydn's funeral mass, at which Carpani was not present, having fled for the second time before the approaching French army of Napoleon.

Beyle, like Carpani, gives his letters fictitious dates, and in so doing he commits the fatal error of referring to Napoleon's Russian campaign of 1814 in a letter dated June 2, 1809. But his biography may not be written off simply as a plagiarism. Beyle revised Carpani's work, and he shortened, turned about, and improved many of its sentences, a fact to which Larousse's *Dictionnaire universel du XIX⁰ siècle* has already called attention.

In this matter Carpani had another opinion. In two open letters of August 1815 to the *Giornale dell' italiana letteratura* he vigorously attacks Bombet, denies that he was personally acquainted with Haydn, and accuses him of lying and of stealing intellectual property. Bombet, for his part, accuses Carpani of plagiarism in a reply to the journal *Constitutionel,* and in his last response goes so far as to represent himself as his own brother who was too old and too gouty to concern himself further with music and Carpani.

Despite the many discrepancies, these two biographies must not be rejected *in toto*. The remark that in *The Creation* the pizzicato that precedes the line "und es ward Licht" (and there was light) represents the Eternal Father striking flint against stone and producing a spark in the darkness can certainly be attributed to Haydn. All that Carpani says of Haydn's ancestors is that they were born, lived, and then died, but this brief account is plainer and more concise than everything that is written on the subject today, however good it may be. Genius cannot be explained by heredity.

Though Stendhal saw only Haydn's catafalque, Carl Bertuch met the master, while he was still alive on a trip to Vienna in 1805–6. In 1806 he visited Haydn 12 times, and in 1808 at Weimar he published his *Bemerkungen* about these meetings. During his last visit, on December 20, Haydn promised him a catalog of his works. This is the well-known Elssler Catalog. At the end of Bertuch's version we find 400 minuets and German dances that are to be found neither in the original nor in any of the copies, but Bertuch cannot have invented it himself. He then offers a brief biographical sketch that agrees with the beginning of Griesinger's notice. This is the reason why I earlier expressed the opinion that by 1806 Griesinger himself had not progressed further with his biography.

In the program booklet for a performance of *The Creation* that he conducted during Lent 1809, in Bergamo, Giovanni Simone Mayr wrote a brief notice about Haydn's life and works. This performance, incidentally, was the first occasion on which the work was heard in Italy in its entirety. The notice itself was the first biographical sketch of Haydn. In it Mayr maintained that Haydn had told him that the degree of skill which caused Count Morzin to hire him had been reached only through tireless diligence exerted without the aid of a teacher or master. This does not agree with his mention of Porpora as his teacher in his autobiographical sketch. The date when Mayr met Haydn has not yet been determined. In any case, Mayr is not among the visitors of the last years of Haydn's life who are listed by Botstiber in the third volume of the Pohl biography.

If, in situations in which a direct contact between Haydn and an author can be proved, statements are made that cannot be clarified, how much worse is the situation with regard to the utterances of writers who did not know Haydn personally! We can show this by examining the orations delivered in his memory at the Institut de France, of which Haydn was a foreign member. De Framery and Le Breton delivered addresses which, aside from a few already well-known facts about Haydn's life, consisted entirely of anecdotes based primarily on oral statements by Pleyel and Neukomm. Yet in both of them we already find mention of Spangler, who is said to have harbored Haydn after his discharge from the choir school. Pohl later repeated this.

The Institut speeches were published in 1810. Griesinger, reviewing Le Breton's address in the *Allgemeine musikalische Zeitung* of February 20, 1811, makes the important remark that many of the anecdotes, as Haydn told them himself, sounded completely different from the subsequent versions. Dies also remarks that Haydn, when telling stories of his life, gave his mood of the moment free play. These stories were thus subject to variation! But this is no excuse for Carpani's bombastic decorations. Fantastic rumors occurred even during Haydn's lifetime. As the Newberry Library in Chicago informed me the other day, *Poulson's American Daily Advertiser* for March 7, 1805, carried this announcement in Philadelphia: "Died, at Vienna, the beginning of December, the celebrated composer, Haydn, in the 79th year of his age." Haydn lived until 1809 but did not reach the age of 79!

In the next 65 years there appeared larger and smaller biographies of Haydn, some of which I have been able to study in the Music Division of this Library. One of these, the work of Franz Joseph Fröhlich, was published in the Ersch and Gruber encyclopedia of 1820. It contains the crudest falsifications; yet Sandberger reprinted it in 1936 at a time when no one was yet thinking about new editions of the vastly more important biographies by Griesinger and Dies. The other biographies, among which are those by C. Albert Ludwig and H. Barbedette (appearing when Pohl had already begun work on his Haydn biography), are as good as forgotten.

Scholarly Haydn research dates its true beginning from 1878, when the first volume of the biography by Carl Ferdinand Pohl appeared. He went back to the sources and winnowed the available material according to strict historical criteria. His biography of Haydn was conceived on a wide scale. It is the first such study to devote attention to Haydn's wife and his circle of friends, two matters about which Haydn himself did not report. Beyond this, Pohl reserved considerable space for discussions of the musical life of the time and general social relationships, as indeed he had done in an earlier special study of Haydn's London period. Although he gives detailed descriptions of Vienna, Eisenstadt, and Esterháza, and the kind of life led by the reigning princes, Haydn is always at the center of the story.

Though Pohl errs in the exact date of that touching farewell scene that I have already discussed, he sets Haydn's departure for Hainburg in the right year, 1737. This was the year in which Michael Haydn was born, and it is the year in which Haydn himself placed the trip in his autobiographical sketch. Then Pohl shows that Reutter could not have come to Hainburg prior to 1739 because he did not take over the supervision of the choirboys until the death of his father in the fall of 1738. Since Griesinger associates the encounter of Reutter and Haydn with cherries, it must have taken place early in the summer.

In the autobiographical sketch Haydn writes: "When I was seven years old the late Herr Kapellmeister von Reutter fortuitously learned of my weak but pleasant voice." But we must bear in mind that in this sketch Haydn placed his birth date one year too late. When Reutter heard him, he must therefore have been not seven but eight years old, the age he would indeed have been in 1739. Haydn then continues: "He [Reutter] immediately took me into the choir school." Pohl corrects this. Haydn did not go to Vienna until the end of his eighth year—that is, in 1740.

Pohl places Haydn's discharge from St. Stephen's in 1749. He then has Haydn meet the tenor Spangler, who takes him into his poor quarters until Haydn sets out on his pilgrimage to Mariazell. Haydn did not mention Spangler in his conversations with his visitors, but 40 years later he supported Spangler's children, which indicates that he was obligated to the singer. Even in his old age, Haydn never forgot the good deeds done him in his youth, a fact also proved by his will.

Pohl writes that he had the greatest difficulty with the chronological order of events in the years immediately following Haydn's discharge from St. Stephen's. We are still in the same position today, and we must not find fault with Pohl for not having always succeeded in reconciling the crisscrossing contradictions of the earlier biographies. He carefully examined all of these biographies and pointed out many discrepancies. But he himself fell victim to several, for example, that regarding Haydn's visit in Bad Mannersdorf.

Porpora traveled to Bad Mannersdorf in the company of the Venetian ambassador Correr and his mistress whose singing teacher he was. Porpora is supposed to have brought Haydn along as his servant to function as accompanist for these singing lessons. In Mannersdorf, Haydn, who was then about 20 years old, is supposed to have met Gluck and Wagenseil and to have had a meeting with Dittersdorf. In a concert given by the Prince of Sachsen-Hildburghausen, Dittersdorf is said to have hoaxed the ambassador while he was playing the violin. In Dittersdorf's autobiography this event takes place several years later in the fall during the vintage. In summer the Prince of Sachsen-Hildburghausen resided and gave concerts on his estate, Schlosshof, until he sold it to Emperor Franz.

Pohl's biography also tells how, at a rehearsal in Paris in 1789, Gyrowetz placed before the orchestra a symphony of his own which had previously been known under Haydn's name. Many years later Gyrowetz wrote in his autobiography that the symphony in question had been published by Schlesinger. Pohl accepts this supposed fact without objection, though in 1789 there was no music publishing house of Schlesinger. About 10 years later in Munich, Gyrowetz again heard the symphony and again it was offered as a work by Haydn. I have not been able to identify the symphony in question.

Pohl is also in error when he lists Willmann among the Paris publishers of Haydn's works and has Haydn act as his own publisher for the piano sonatas nos. 40, 41, and 42. In the first volume of my Haydn catalog I have corrected all this, as well as Pohl's erroneous assertion that the published parts of the first version of *The Seven Last Words* contain the introductory bass recitatives. These recitatives are part of Frieberth's arrangement of the work, an arrangement that Haydn heard in Passau while on his second journey to England.

Pohl describes in detail this journey as well as Haydn's first trip to London, when he traveled via Bonn. We do not know when Haydn began the return voyage from his first stay in London. In his letters he repeatedly wrote that he intended to leave at the end of June 1792. But the last of the letters that Mrs. Schroeter wrote to him can be interpreted to mean that he was still in London on July 2, for in it Mrs. Schroeter invites him to dinner on that day.

The trip to Bonn would have taken six or seven days. He met the music publisher Simrock there and negotiated with him about the publication of symphonies. Botstiber's assumption that the Elector's orchestra tendered Haydn a dinner on this occasion in the Redoutensaal of the neighboring town of Godesberg—a dinner at which he is supposed to have met Beethoven—probably rests on a confusion with the dinner Prince-Elector Maximilian Franz gave Haydn in Bonn, when he passed through this city in December 1790 on his first journey to London. I could find no evidence of such a Godesberg dinner in contemporary local papers as far as they are preserved. Besides this, Pohl does not mention such a dinner in his essay on Haydn in London. As for Beethoven, by the summer of 1790 he had finished the cantata on the death of Emperor Joseph II, which he is supposed to have shown to Haydn during that dinner. He is more likely to have shown Haydn the cantata in December of that same year than on Haydn's return from England two years later. Moreover, Beethoven's cantata on the elevation of Emperor Leopold II was also completed in 1790.

In another letter Haydn writes that he wants to travel to Frankfurt am Main because his Prince expects him there for the coronation of Emperor Franz II on July 14. It was not the then reigning Prince Paul Anton who went to Frankfurt, but his son, the later Nicolaus II. Nicolaus took with him only a small part of the musical organization and would scarcely have needed Haydn. On the other hand, there is a letter of the Mainz publisher Bernhard Schott, who had already visited Haydn in Bonn on the journey to England. According to this letter, Schott met Haydn in Biebrich on July 17, after having been notified of Haydn's arrival by Simrock in Bonn. But if Haydn, traveling from Bonn, first arrived in Biebrich on July 17, he cannot have been at the coronation in Frankfurt on July 14. The rest of his route is not known. In any case, he was back in Vienna on July 24.

On the second return trip Haydn traveled via Hamburg but not to visit C. P. E. Bach, as we are told, for Bach had died on December 14, 1788, and Haydn must have definitely been aware of this. Furthermore, he had been expected in Hamburg by the bookdealer Westphal ever since his first English trip. He is supposed to have presented to the Hamburgers a melody for trumpet which thereafter was played from the tower of a church. But this may also be merely an anecdote.

Haydn left London on August 15, 1795, and a notice in a Hamburg paper states that he arrived in that city on August 19. This arrival would have taken place in the evening, for the correspondent of an English paper did not report the event to London until the following day. Since Haydn could not have taken the Calais route because of the Franco-Austrian war, he must have traveled by sea. As it happens there left, on that very day, a direct passenger ship from Harwich to Hamburg. However, direct proof has not been discovered that Haydn was actually aboard this ship, together with his amanuensis Elssler, who had accompanied him on his second journey, and presumably also the parrot he was given in England.

Despite many errors and gaps, Pohl's biography remains the single fundamental work on which all subsequent serious Haydn biographies are based. Thus it is incomprehensible that four years after

19

the publication of Pohl's first volume there appeared *Joseph Haydn, ein Lebensbild* by Franz von Seeburg (a pseudonym for Franz Hacker), a book that makes a mockery of all the preceding biographies. Seeburg alters previous depictions—insofar as he makes use of them at all—completely mixes up all matters of chronology, has events occur in the wrong places, and reduces them to sentimentality. The chapter headings show this: "Poor days—good hearts," "It should not have been," "Beggar and bridegroom," "Poor as a churchmouse," "It is all in God's hands," "The shimmering bubble of luck bursts," and many more. This book, which later appeared with the subtitle "The Novel of an Artist," went into its seventh edition as late as 1929. In 1888 it was translated into French, and within two years this translation went through four editions.

After the recent war the book was made available in condensed form in the series *Deutsches Gut,* but it was shortly replaced by a popular novel by Heinrich Eduard Jacob. Though more soundly based and better written than Seeburg's book, Jacob's novel also contains freely invented sentimental episodes which follow in Carpani's steps. Jacob even outdoes Carpani in citing the names of artists. The anecdotes are expanded to short stories, and at the very outset the book offers an anecdote that was not previously heard. According to this tale, a poor Austrian farmer set about bringing his cow into her stall on a warm summer day in 1735. He shrank back when he clearly heard a mooing in the stable and perceived that something was moving in the straw. He thought that the devil had conjured a second cow, crossed himself, and fled in terror to the priest. The priest examined the stable and found not magic, but a three-year-old child playing cow. The excited reader is surprised by the *dénouement.* The child is none other than Joseph Haydn who, in his earliest youth, is clearly adumbrating the animal imitations of his late, great oratorios. This book first appeared in New York in 1950. A year later it was translated into French, accompanied by a laudatory preface by Thomas Mann which also accompanies the German edition of 1952. Then it was brought out by the Gutenberg Book Club, and ever since it has been among the most discussed books about Haydn.

I should not have mentioned these two books were it not for the fact that they have definitely contributed to a diminution of the picture of Haydn among a wide circle of readers and thereby increased public preference for pieces like the "Toy Symphony," the Ox-Minuet (which Griesinger had attacked), or the serenade from the so-called Opus 3, the authenticity of which is by no means established. But these books at least show a certain love for Father Haydn. This love is completely absent in the historical and psychological study based on an analysis of Haydn's string quartets, published in London in 1951 by Robert Sondheimer. The author disintegrates the quartets into tiny melodic scraps to prove that these are all to be found in works by earlier composers, who, moreover, use them in a more coherent fashion. He then accuses Haydn of having combined these scraps for mercantile reasons into works of rhythmical ebullience, after having drained them of their intense emotional poetry—thus is it expressed in the English version of this study, which was translated from the German.

It is inconceivable that Haydn should be accused of such a thing, for he especially made derogatory comments about contemporaries who put one little bit of music after another and broke off when they scarcely had begun.

Sondheimer further pretends that Haydn's string quartets first led the way in music to the ominous separation of Art and Life, and that they are no longer "fraught with immense feelings as in the pre-classics" who, in Sondheimer's own words, sought essential nature and not external splendor in music. Considering, according to Haydn's own words, that a musical composition should consist of flowing song and integrated ideas in order to reach the hearer's heart through its continuity, one might conclude that he would not have had much use for the "immense feelings" that Sondheimer misses in his music.

In conclusion, I return to the beginning of my lecture and the remark I made that we really know very little about Haydn's life, at least in comparison with what we know about the lives of Mozart, Beethoven, Schubert, and other composers. Our first glimpse into Haydn's private life comes from his correspondence with Frau von

21

Genzinger, which begins with a letter of June 10, 1789, when he was 57 years old. The correspondence becomes ever more ardent on Haydn's side. On one occasion he even felt obliged to reassure the noble lady that a letter to her, which went astray, did not contain anything that could compromise her.

Haydn carried on this correspondence during his first stay in London, but his most ardent letters from that period are addressed to Luigia Polzelli. She was engaged at the Esterházy opera in 1779 but was soon dismissed because of her mediocrity as a singer. It was through Haydn's own special request that Prince Nicolaus kept her at Esterháza. As a result we have been bestowed with several fine arias which Haydn especially composed for her as insertions in operas that were performed there under his direction.

In one of the letters to Polzelli, Haydn calls his wife an infernal beast. Probably she had communicated to him some unpleasant things about Polzelli, and she may have been perfectly right in doing so. The Italian singer directed much of her attention towards money, and a few weeks after Haydn's death she attempted to obtain an annuity from his estate on the basis of a declaration made by him nine years earlier. Haydn, however, revoked this declaration and had her cut out of his last will. He probably decided that she had already obtained enough from him during his lifetime.

Although we do not know much about Haydn's mistress, we know still less about his wife. He married her after the termination of his employment with Count Morzin and before he entered the service of Prince Esterházy. He had really wanted to marry her sister who, however, became a nun. But if, on the one hand, Haydn's wife is accused of bigotry and extravagance and of having rolled up Haydn's autographs in order to use them as hair curlers, other biographers write that she well and truly accompanied him on his trips to Vienna.

As I have said, we do not know where she stayed or what she did while Haydn was at Esterháza with Polzelli. Even the latest research, done for me on this point in Vienna, brought no results. After the death of Prince Nicolaus, Haydn moved to an apartment which his wife is supposed to have occupied in Vienna. He lived with her there between his two English journeys, and they moved together into his house in Gumpendorf after he remodeled it. He also carried on a correspondence with her from London. It is another remarkable fate of Haydn research that, while letters to Frau von Genzinger and Luigia Polzelli have been preserved, there is no trace whatever of Haydn's correspondence with his wife.

Judged by her will, she was more primitive than malicious or evil. On one occasion Haydn refused a present intended for her. He loved his wife, he argued, but she wanted for nothing and had performed no service that warranted recompense. On another occasion he is supposed to have said of her that it would have been all the same to her whether her husband had been a composer or a shoemaker. He kept a picture of her until his death, but the picture has disappeared. He showed it to one of his last visitors with the comment: "That is my wife. She has often enraged me," which, in general, is not so uncommon.

I could go on for a considerable time telling you about discrepancies I have found in Haydn biographies while consulting them during my researches for my Haydn catalog. This would come very near to the scope of a new Haydn biography which, however, I do not intend to write. I must finish the catalog; but I hope I have shown you to what extent biographical researches are necessary before completion can be contemplated.

U.S. GOVERNMENT PRINTING OFFICE: 1962